Cotton Way Classics

Fresh Quilts for a Charming Home

BONNIE OLAVESON

Martingale®
Create with Confidence

Cotton Way Classics:
Fresh Quilts for a Charming Home
© 2017 by Bonnie Olaveson

Martingale®
19021 120th Ave. NE, Ste. 102
Bothell, WA 98011-9511 USA
ShopMartingale.com

Printed in China
22 21 20 19 18 17   8 7 6 5 4 3 2 1

**Library of Congress Cataloging-in-Publication Data
is available on request.**

ISBN: 978-1-60468-878-8

MISSION STATEMENT

We empower makers who use fabric and yarn
to make life more enjoyable.

CREDITS

**PUBLISHER AND
CHIEF VISIONARY OFFICER**
Jennifer Erbe Keltner

CONTENT DIRECTOR
Karen Costello Soltys

MANAGING EDITOR
Tina Cook

ACQUISITIONS EDITOR
Karen M. Burns

TECHNICAL EDITOR
Elizabeth Beese

COPY EDITOR
Sheila Chapman Ryan

DESIGN MANAGER
Adrienne Smitke

PRODUCTION MANAGER
Regina Girard

**COVER AND
INTERIOR DESIGNER**
Angie Hoogensen

PHOTOGRAPHER
Brent Kane

ILLUSTRATOR
Sandy Huffaker

SPECIAL THANKS
*Thanks to Suzie and Bernhard Bauer of Snohomish,
Washington; Lynn Austin of Kirkland, Washington; and
Jim and Heidi Minick of Ann Arbor, Michigan, for allowing
the photography for this book to take place in their homes.*

contents

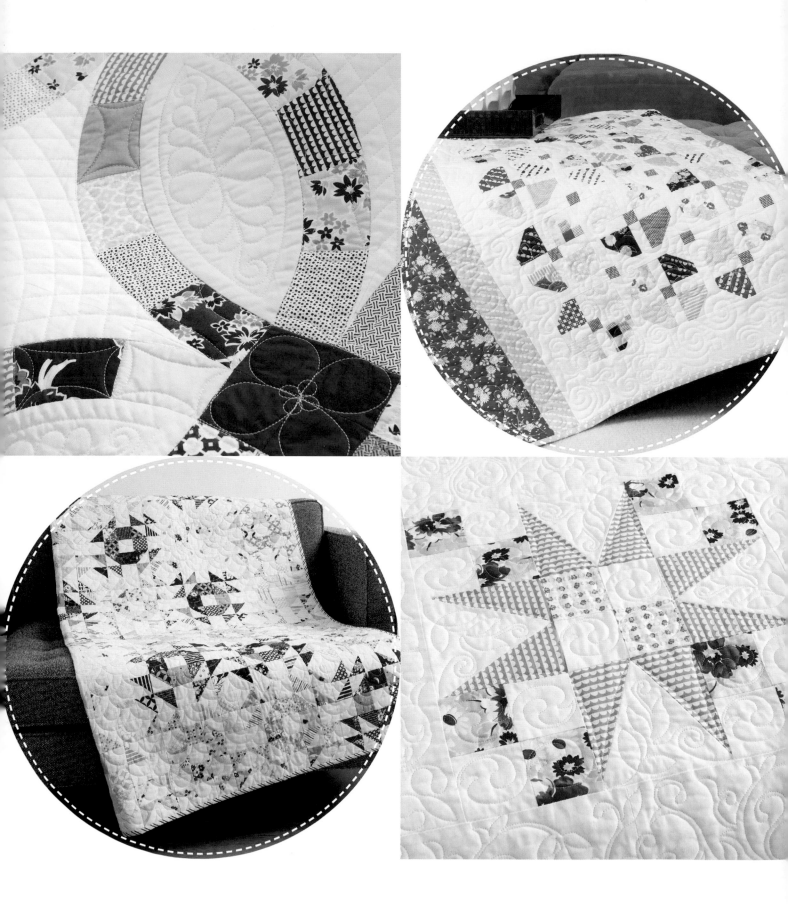

introduction

Growing up in a family where quilting has been a long-standing tradition, there's nothing I like better than sewing with one of my 17 grandchildren—or snuggling under a cozy quilt with them!

As a child, I remember my Grandma Sarah hand quilting, and my 90-year-old Mom still pieces and hand quilts. My mother taught me to sew when I was just six, and I have been designing, cutting up fabric, and sewing ever since. I studied pattern design in college, never dreaming it would take me where I am today.

It's hard to imagine that it's been almost 30 years (and 400 patterns!) since I started my design company, Cotton Way. My husband, Mark, and I raised five kids, and they all grew up folding patterns, helping to fill and ship orders, and even offering opinions about what I was working on. My daughter, Camille, now runs her own design company, Thimble Blossoms, and together, we design fabric for Moda Fabrics under the name Bonnie and Camille.

I still love being able to go into my studio to cut and stitch, press, and bind. Those tasks have helped me through some of my roughest days and given my hands something to do when I needed it most. The quilts in this book are among my very favorite—a few are more traditional, others have a modern twist. I hope they will help you to find that creative gift inside of you and that you enjoy the process of making them.

Most of the projects are scrappy, and I've used our Bonnie and Camille fabric in each one. Don't be afraid to change the colorway, mix up the backgrounds, and make each quilt your own. Fill your home with handmade quilts that will surely give your home a happy, warm, and inviting charm.

~ *Bonnie*

Cut up charm squares and piece them back together to make multicolored blocks that look like spinning tops. Colorful borders are sewn to the quilt sides only, adding some whimsy to the quilt design.

topsy turvy

QUILT SIZE: 57¾" × 61¾"
BLOCK SIZE: 4¾" × 4¾"

MATERIALS

Yardage is based on 42"-wide fabric, except as noted. Charm squares are 5" × 5".

- 70 charm squares of assorted prints and stripes for blocks
- 2¾ yards of white solid for block backgrounds, sashing, and inner border
- ¼ yard of red print A for cornerstones
- ⅞ yard of green diagonal stripe for middle side borders and binding
- ⅞ yard of red print B for outer side borders
- 3⅝ yards of fabric for backing
- 64" × 68" piece of batting

CUTTING

All measurements include ¼" seam allowances.

From the white solid, cut:

2 strips, 4" × 42"

4 strips, 2½" × 42"

13 strips, 1¾" × 42"; crosscut into 280 squares, 1¾" × 1¾"

37 strips, 1¼" × 42"; crosscut into:
    123 rectangles, 1¼" × 5¼"
    280 rectangles, 1¼" × 2½"

From red print A, cut:

4 strips, 1¼" × 42"; crosscut into 124 squares, 1¼" × 1¼"

From the green diagonal stripe, cut:

11 strips, 2½" × 42"

From red print B, cut:

4 strips, 6¼" × 42"

MAKING THE BLOCKS

Sew pieces right sides together. Press all seam allowances as indicated by the arrows.

1. Using a pencil and ruler, mark a diagonal line from corner to corner on the wrong side of each white square.

2. Place a white square on the corner of a print square, right sides together, and stitch on the marked line. Trim the excess corner fabric, leaving a ¼" seam allowance. Press. Repeat, sewing a white square to each corner of the print square. Repeat for all 70 print squares.

Make 70 units,
5" × 5".

7

Designed and pieced by **BONNIE OLAVESON;** machine quilted by **LEANN POWELL**

3 Cut each print square into quarters vertically and horizontally as shown. Each unit should be 2½" square.

4 Choose four different prints from step 3 for each block. Lay out the units with one red print A square and four white 1¼" × 2½" rectangles. Sew the pieces together in rows; press. Join the rows to complete the block, which should measure 5¼" square, including the seam allowances. Make 70.

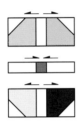

Make 70 blocks, 5¼" × 5¼".

ASSEMBLING THE QUILT TOP

1 Lay out the blocks in 10 rows of seven blocks per row, leaving space between the blocks for the white 1¼" × 5¼" rectangles. Add the white rectangles vertically in each block row and horizontally between the block rows. Lay out the remaining red A squares between the horizontal white strips.

2 Sew the pieces in each block row together and press. Sew the pieces in each sashing row together and press. Join the block and sashing rows to complete the quilt-top center, which should measure 38¼" × 54¾".

3 For the white top and bottom borders, measure the width of the quilt top. Trim each white 4"-wide strip to this length, which should be 38¼". Sew one strip to the top and the other to the bottom of the quilt. Press.

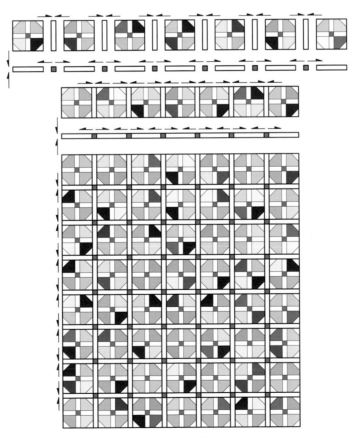

Quilt assembly

4 To make the white side borders, sew two of the white 2½"-wide strips together end to end. Repeat to make a second border strip. Measure the length of the quilt top and trim both border strips to this length, which should be 61¾". Sew the border strips to the sides of the quilt. Press.

5 For the green side borders, repeat step 4 using the green stripe 2½"-wide strips. Press.

6 For the red side borders, repeat step 4 using the 6¼"-wide red print B strips. Press.

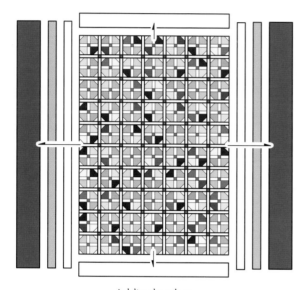

Adding borders

FINISHING THE QUILT

For more explanation on any of the finishing steps, go to ShopMartingale.com/HowtoQuilt for free downloadable information.

1 Prepare the quilt backing so it's about 6" larger in both directions than the quilt top.

2 Layer the backing (right side down), batting, and quilt top (right side up). Baste the layers together.

3 Hand or machine quilt; the quilt shown is quilted with an allover swirl-and-flower design.

4 Use the remaining green stripe 2½"-wide strips to make binding and attach it to the quilt.

Bonnie Says: I've always loved scrappy quilts, so charm squares are one of my favorite precuts. Using a variety of charm squares gives quilts a scrappier look than if you'd made the same pattern from just a few fat quarters or big cuts of yardage. Plus, charm squares minimize cutting!

lazy days

What looks like set-in seams on these blocks are actually stitch-and-flip corners. The cheery red gingham brings to mind relaxing summer days and indulgent picnics.

QUILT SIZE: 72" × 72"
BLOCK SIZE: 6" × 6"

MATERIALS

Yardage is based on 42"-wide fabric.

- 3⅝ yards of white solid for background and borders
- 1⅛ yards of red gingham for blocks and binding
- 4 pieces, ½ yard *each,* of assorted red prints for blocks
- 5 pieces, ½ yard *each,* of assorted aqua prints for blocks
- ¾ yard of red dot for border
- 4⅜ yards of fabric for backing
- 78" × 78" piece of batting

CUTTING

All measurements include ¼" seam allowances.

From the white solid, cut:
10 strips, 7½" × 42"; crosscut into 50 squares, 7½" × 7½". Cut each square into quarters diagonally to make 200 triangles.

3 strips, 3" × 42"; crosscut into 28 squares, 3" × 3"

8 strips, 2¼" × 42"

7 strips, 2" × 42"

From the red gingham, cut:
1 strip, 7" × 42"; crosscut into 5 squares, 7" × 7". Cut each square in half diagonally to make 10 triangles.

2 strips, 3" × 42"; crosscut into 20 squares, 3" × 3"

8 strips, 2½" × 42"

From *each* red print and aqua print, cut:
1 strip, 7" × 42"; crosscut into 5 squares, 7" × 7" (45 total). Cut each square in half diagonally to make 90 triangles.

2 strips, 3" × 42"; crosscut into 20 squares, 3" × 3" (180 total)

From the red dot, cut:
1 strip, 21½" × 42"; crosscut into 12 strips, 3" × 21½"

MAKING THE BLOCKS

Sew pieces right sides together. Press all seam allowances as indicated by the arrows.

1. Using a pencil and ruler, mark a diagonal line from corner to corner on the wrong side of each red gingham, red print, and aqua square.

2. Place a marked square on the corner of a white triangle, right sides together, and stitch on the marked line. Trim the excess corner fabric, leaving a ¼" seam allowance. Press. Repeat for all 200 white triangles.

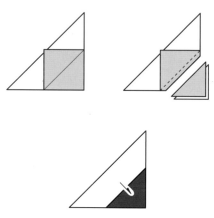

Make 200.

3. Sew together two matching triangles from step 2 to make a pieced triangle. Press the seam allowances open. Sew a matching red or aqua triangle to the pieced triangle to make a block; press. Trim the block to measure 6½" square, including seam allowances. Make 100 blocks total (50 red and 50 aqua).

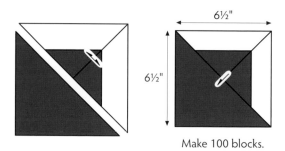

Make 100 blocks.

Designed and pieced by **BONNIE OLAVESON;** machine quilted by **SUSAN HANSEN**

ASSEMBLING THE QUILT TOP

1. Lay out the blocks in 10 rows of 10 blocks per row, alternating between red and aqua blocks. Make sure the red blocks and the aqua blocks are in the correct place and facing in the correct direction. I arranged my blocks in pairs of matching red blocks going diagonally in one direction and pairs of matching aqua blocks going in the opposite direction.

2. Sew the blocks in each row together. Press. Join the block rows to complete the quilt-top center, which should measure 60½" square. Press.

3. For the inner border, stitch the white 2"-wide strips together end to end and press the seam allowances open. Cut two border strips, 60½" long. Sew the border strips to opposite edges of the quilt. Press. Cut two border strips, 63½" long, and sew them to the remaining edges of the quilt. Press.

4. Using a pencil and ruler, mark a diagonal line from corner to corner on the wrong side of 24 of the white squares.

5. Place a marked square on one end of a red dot 3" × 21½" strip, right sides together, and stitch on the marked line. Trim the excess corner fabric, leaving a ¼" seam allowance. Press. Add another marked square to the other end of the red strip, making sure the diagonal line is facing the correct direction. Repeat for all 12 red dot strips.

Make 12 strips,
3" × 21½".

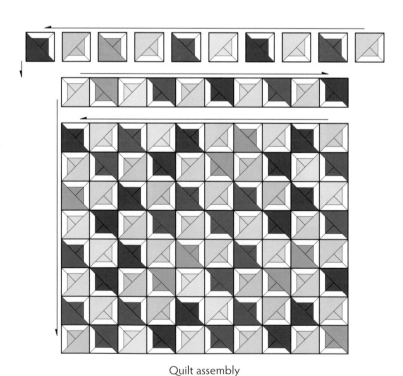

Quilt assembly

6 For the red middle border, stitch three strips from step 5 together; press the seam allowances open. Repeat to make four middle-border strips. Each border strip should measure 63½" long. Sew two middle-border strips to opposite sides of the quilt, making sure the pieced diagonal sections are facing the correct direction as shown below; press. Stitch a white 3" square to both ends of each remaining border strip; press. Sew these border strips to the top and bottom of the quilt; press.

7 For the outer border, sew the white 2¼"-wide strips together end to end; press the seam allowances open. Measure the width of the quilt top, which should now be 68½", and cut two border strips to this length. Sew the border strips to opposite edges of the quilt top. Press.

8 Measure the length of the quilt top, which should now be 72", and cut two border strips to this length. Sew the border strips to the remaining edges of the quilt top. Press.

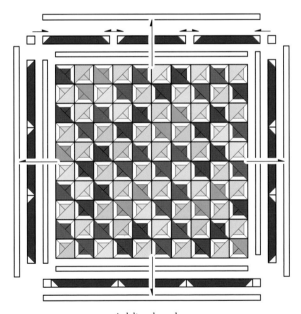

Adding borders

FINISHING THE QUILT

For more explanation on any of the finishing steps, go to ShopMartingale.com/HowtoQuilt for free downloadable information.

1 Prepare the quilt backing so it's about 6" larger in both directions than the quilt top.

2 Layer the backing (right side down), batting, and quilt top (right side up). Baste the layers together.

3 Hand or machine quilt; the quilt shown is quilted with an allover pattern of double interlocking circles.

4 Use the red gingham 2½"-wide strips to make binding and attach it to the quilt.

Bonnie Says: Making blocks from pieces you'd tossed into your scrap basket would yield a very different, yet charming, version of the Lazy Days quilt. It's always wonderful to find a home for those last little bits of your favorite fabrics you can't seem to get enough of.

If you've ever wanted to make a Double Wedding Ring quilt but have been intimidated, try this version. It's put together with a simple block-to-block construction and the curves in the large blocks are gentle.

kate's big day

 QUILT SIZE: 72½" × 72½"
BLOCK SIZE: 12" × 12"

MATERIALS

Yardage is based on 42"-wide fabric, except as noted. Fat eighths are 9" × 21".

- 30 fat eighths of assorted prints for blocks
- 3⅛ yards of white solid for block backgrounds*
- 2 yards of aqua solid for block centers
- ½ yard of red solid for blocks
- ⅝ yard of aqua stripe for binding
- 4½ yards of fabric for backing
- 79" × 79" piece of batting
- Lightweight template plastic
- Fabric marker

If you prefer a more traditional look, cut the block center petals from white solid. You won't need additional fabric, but you'll need to use precise cutting; see "The White Stuff" below.

The White Stuff

To make block petals white instead of aqua, carefully cut the corner pieces from each 10¼" × 11" rectangle. You'll have enough white in the center for one petal piece, so no need for extra yardage.

CUTTING

All measurements include ¼" seam allowances. The arc section, petal, and corner patterns are on pages 21 and 22. The corner pattern is in two pieces; line up the dashed lines when tracing to make one full pattern. See "Making and Using Plastic Templates" on page 26 to make plastic templates from the patterns. To match shapes when piecing, make a tiny (¹⁄₁₆") clip into the edge of each shape where indicated on the pattern.

From *each* fat eighth, cut:
12 ring sections using the pattern (360 total)

From the white solid, cut:
9 strips, 11" × 42"; crosscut into 36 rectangles, 10¼" × 11". From each rectangle, refer to the diagram below to cut 2 corners using the pattern (72 total).

From the aqua solid, cut:
36 petals using the pattern

From the red solid, cut:
5 strips, 2½" × 42"; crosscut into 72 squares, 2½" × 2½"

From the aqua stripe, cut:
8 strips, 2½" × 42"

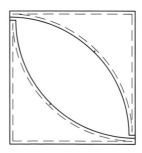

Cutting diagram

MAKING THE BLOCKS

Sew pieces right sides together. Press all seam allowances as indicated by the arrows.

1 Stitch five arc sections together to complete an arc. Press the seam allowances in one direction (it doesn't matter which way). Repeat to make 72 arcs.

Make 72.

2 Match the clip in the middle arc section along the inside edge of an arc with the clip on one side of an aqua petal; pin. Continue pinning around the arc, easing the pieces to fit together. Leave the pins in and carefully stitch over them to make a petal with one arc; press. Repeat to make 36 petals with an arc on one side.

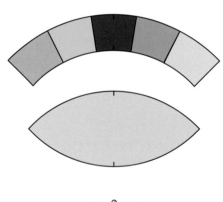

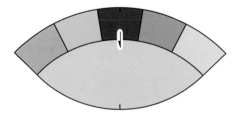

Make 36.

3 Stitch red 2½" squares to both ends of the remaining 36 arcs. Press.

4 Repeat step 2 to sew the arcs with the red squares to the remaining side of the aqua petals, matching the clip marks and the seamlines at the red squares. Press.

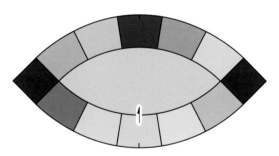

Make 36.

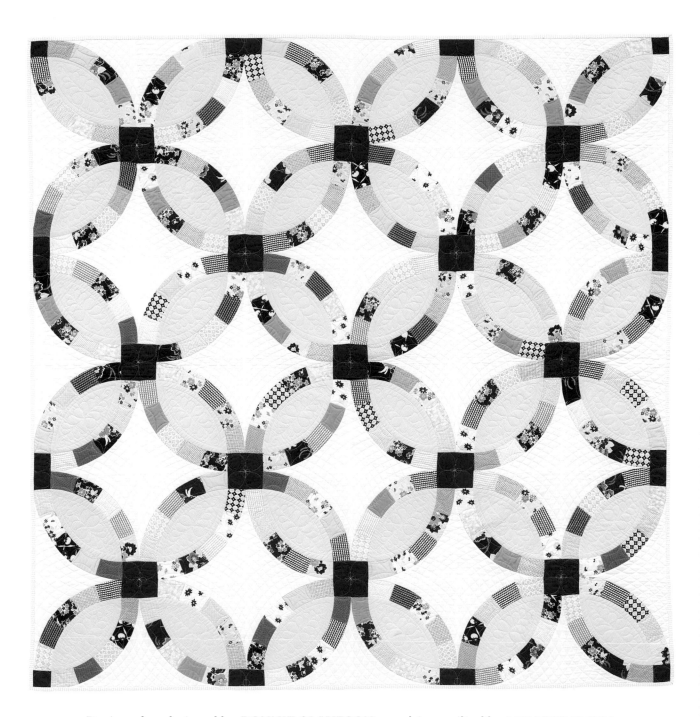

Designed and pieced by **BONNIE OLAVESON**; machine quilted by **LEANN POWELL**

5 Match the center clip of a white corner piece with the clip in the center of the outside edge of an arc; pin. Match the narrow end of each corner piece with the seamline of the red square; pin. Continue pinning around the corner piece's curved edge, easing the pieces to fit together. Leave the pins in and carefully stitch over them. Then remove the pins and press. Repeat to sew a white corner piece to the remaining arc to complete a block, which should measure 12½" square, including the seam allowances. Make 36 blocks.

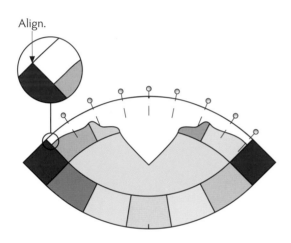

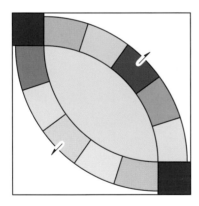

Make 36 blocks,
12½" × 12½".

ASSEMBLING THE QUILT TOP

Lay out the blocks in six rows of six blocks per row. Sew the blocks in each row together and press the seam allowances open. Join the block rows to complete the quilt top, which should measure 72½" × 72½".

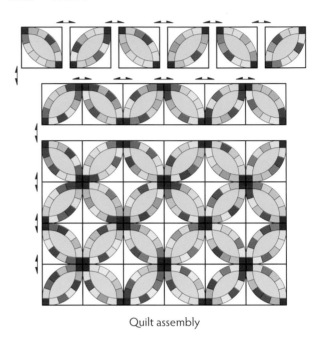

Quilt assembly

FINISHING THE QUILT

For more explanation on any of the finishing steps, go to ShopMartingale.com/HowtoQuilt for free downloadable information.

1 Prepare the quilt backing so it's about 6" larger in both directions than the quilt top.

2 Layer the backing (right side down), batting, and quilt top (right side up). Baste the layers together.

3 Hand or machine quilt; the quilt shown is quilted with curved crosshatching in the white areas, a feathered leaf design in the aqua areas, and curved lines in the ring sections.

4 Use the aqua stripe 2½"-wide strips to make binding and attach it to the quilt.

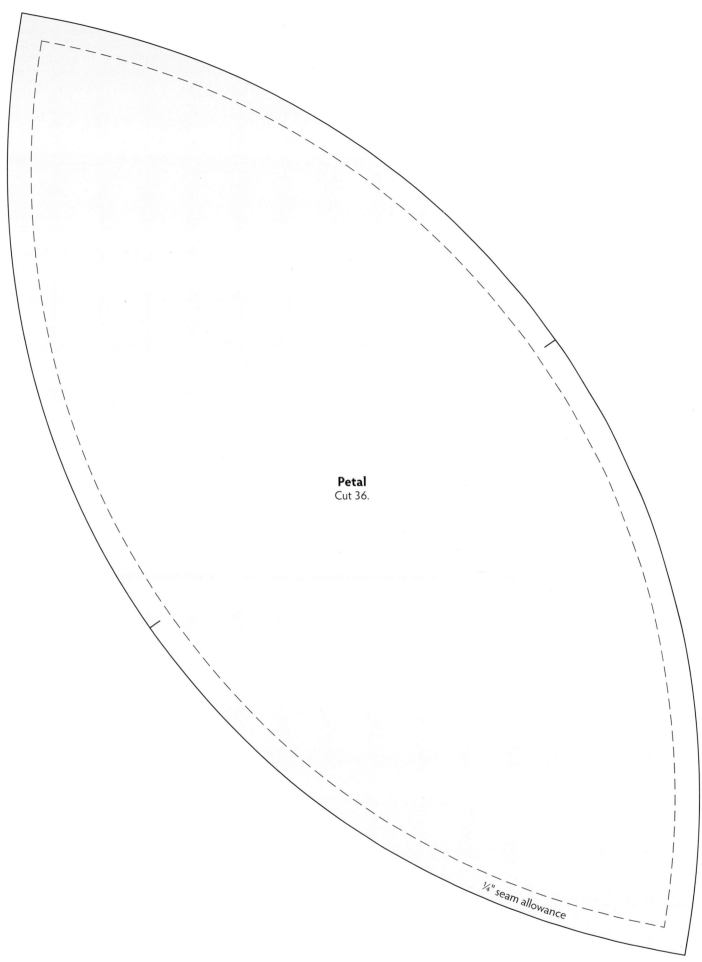

Petal
Cut 36.

¼" seam allowance

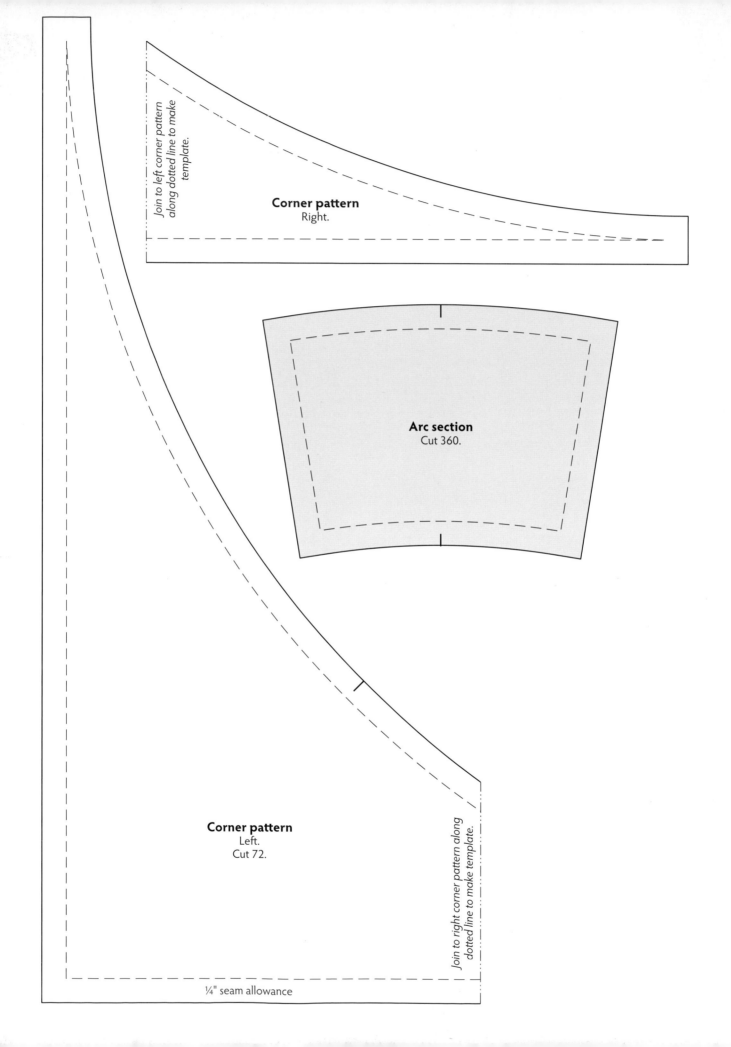

Join to left corner pattern along dotted line to make template.

Corner pattern
Right.

Arc section
Cut 360.

Corner pattern
Left.
Cut 72.

Join to right corner pattern along dotted line to make template.

¼" seam allowance

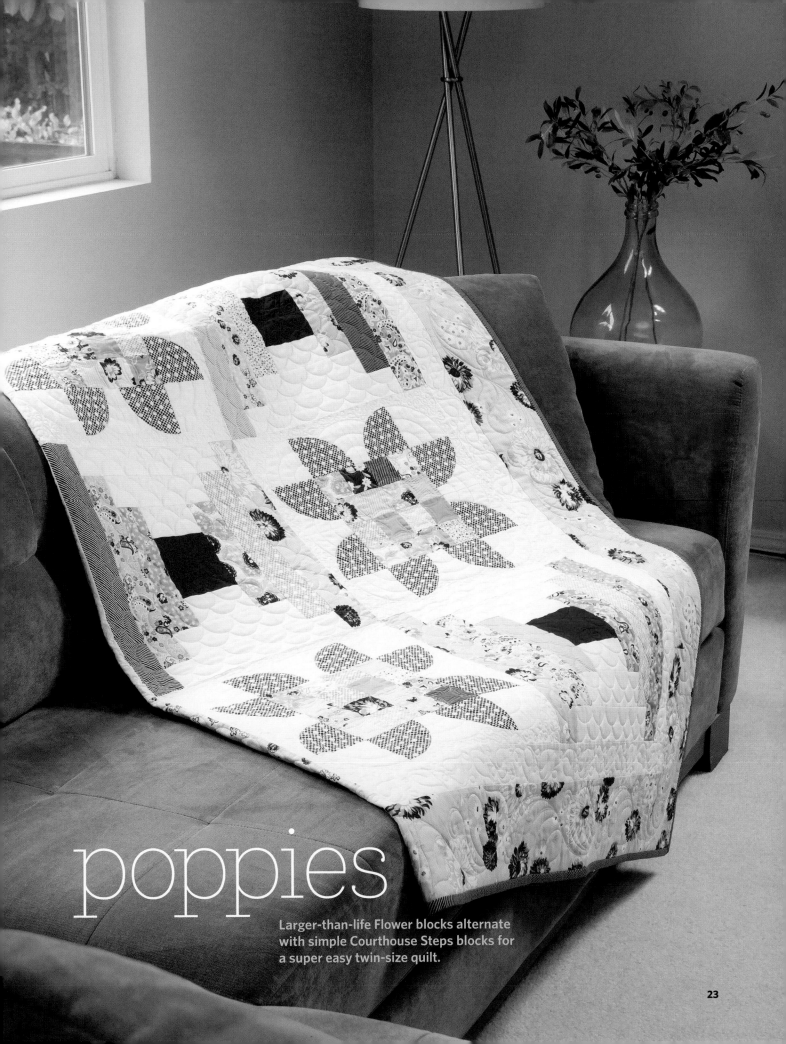

poppies

Larger-than-life Flower blocks alternate
with simple Courthouse Steps blocks for
a super easy twin-size quilt.

 **QUILT SIZE:** 77½" × 93½"
BLOCK SIZE: 16" × 16"

MATERIALS

Yardage is based on 42"-wide fabric.

- 33 to 40 strips, 2½" × 42", of assorted prints for blocks
- 3¾ yards of white solid for block backgrounds and inner border
- 1¼ yards of light red dot for Flower blocks
- ⅓ yard of red solid for Courthouse Steps block centers
- 1⅜ yards of aqua floral for outer border
- ⅞ yard of red stripe for binding
- 7¼ yards of fabric for backing
- 86" × 102" piece of batting
- Lightweight template plastic
- Fabric marker

CUTTING

All measurements include ¼" seam allowances. The petal and petal corner patterns are on page 29. See "Making and Using Plastic Templates" on page 26 to make plastic templates from the patterns.

From the assorted 2½"-wide strips, cut:
20 strips, 2½" × 16½"
20 strips, 2½" × 12½"
20 strips, 2½" × 8½"
160 squares, 2½" × 2½"

From the white solid, cut:
5 strips, 4½" × 42"; crosscut into 40 squares, 4½" × 4½"
14 strips, 2½" × 42"; crosscut into:
    20 strips, 2½" × 12½"
    20 strips, 2½" × 8½"
    20 strips, 2½" × 4½"
8 strips, 2½" × 42"
80 petal corners

From the light red dot, cut:
80 petals

From the red solid, cut:
10 squares, 4½" × 4½"

From the aqua floral, cut:
9 strips, 5" × 42"

From the red stripe, cut:
10 strips, 2½" × 42"

MAKING THE BLOCKS

Sew pieces right sides together. Press all seam allowances as indicated by the arrows.

1. Lay out 16 assorted 2½" squares in four rows of four squares each. Sew together the squares in each row; press. Join the rows to make a 16-patch block center; press. Repeat to make 10 block centers, which should measure 8½" square, including seam allowances.

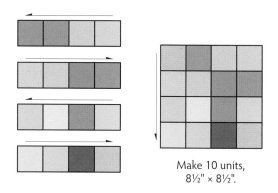

Make 10 units,
8½" × 8½".

2. Pin a white petal corner to a light red dot petal along the curved edge, with the white corner on top. Sew together to make a petal square, which should measure 4½" square, including seam allowances; press. Make 80 petal squares.

Make 80 units,
4½" × 4½".

Designed and pieced by **BONNIE OLAVESON;** machine quilted by **ANDREA MARQUEZ**

3 Making sure they're facing the right direction, sew two petal squares together as shown to make a petal rectangle. Press. Repeat to make 40 petal rectangles.

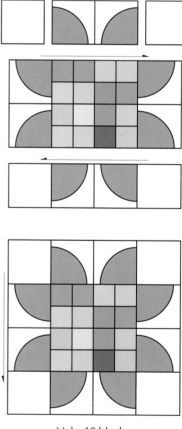

Make 40 units,
4½" × 8½".

4 Lay out four white squares, four petal rectangles, and a block center in three rows as shown. Stitch the pieces in each row; press. Sew the top and bottom rows to the center row to make a Flower block; press. The block should measure 16½" square, including the seam allowances. Make 10 Flower blocks.

Make 10 blocks,
16½" × 16½".

Making and Using Plastic Templates

To make plastic templates, trace the patterns onto lightweight template plastic with a permanent marker and cut them out carefully on the solid lines. To use a template, lay it on the wrong side of the indicated fabric and trace around it with a fabric marker; cut out the fabric shape on the drawn line.

5 Stitch white 2½" × 4½" strips to opposite edges of a red solid square; press. Then stitch assorted 2½" × 8½" strips to the remaining edges of the red square; press. Continue adding strips in the following order, pressing after each addition, to make a Courthouse Steps block: white 2½" × 8½" strips, assorted 2½" × 12½" strips, white 2½" × 12½" strips, and assorted 2½" × 16½" strips. The block should measure 16½" square, including the seam allowances. Make 10 Courthouse Steps blocks.

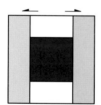
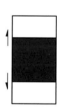
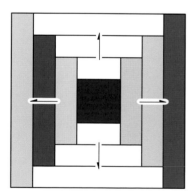

Make 10 blocks,
16½" × 16½".

ASSEMBLING THE QUILT TOP

1. Lay out the blocks in five rows of four blocks per row, alternating the Flower and Courthouse Steps blocks. Sew the blocks in each row together and press. Join the block rows to complete the quilt-top center, which should measure 64½" × 80½".

2. For the inner border, stitch the white 2½"-wide strips together end to end and press the seam allowances open. Measure the width of the quilt top, which should be 64½", and cut two border strips to this length. Sew the border strips to the top and bottom of the quilt. Press.

3. Measure the length of the quilt top, which should now be 84½", and cut two border strips to this length. Sew the border strips to the sides of the quilt. Press.

4. For the outer border, sew the aqua 5"-wide strips together end to end and press the seam allowances open. Measure the width of the quilt top, which should now be 68½", and cut two border strips to this length. Sew the border strips to the top and bottom of the quilt top. Press.

Quilt assembly

5 Measure the length of the quilt top, which should now be 93½", and cut two border strips to this length. Sew the border strips to the sides of the quilt top. Press.

Adding borders

FINISHING THE QUILT

For more explanation on any of the finishing steps, go to ShopMartingale.com/HowtoQuilt for free downloadable information.

1 Prepare the quilt backing so it's about 8" larger in both directions than the quilt top.

2 Layer the backing (right side down), batting, and quilt top (right side up). Baste the layers together.

3 Hand or machine quilt; the quilt shown is quilted with circular designs in the Flower blocks, a clamshell pattern in the Courthouse Steps blocks, and leaves and swirls in the borders.

4 Use the red stripe 2½"-wide strips to make binding and attach it to the quilt.

Bonnie Says: Whether you're working on a simple or a more challenging pattern, being precise in your cutting, stitching an accurate ¼" seam allowance, pressing as you go, and paying attention to details will make you much happier with the finished quilt. This is especially true when you're sewing curved edges. Remember that pinning every ¼" will help you avoid puckers.

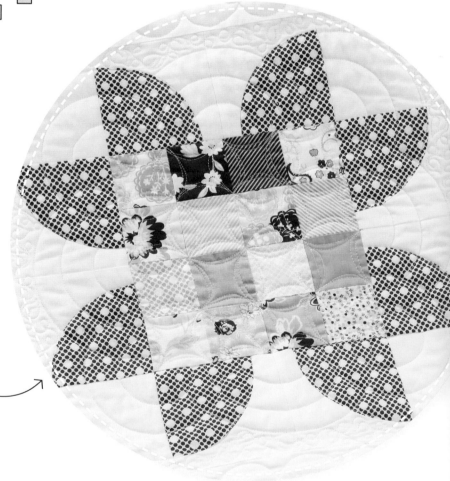

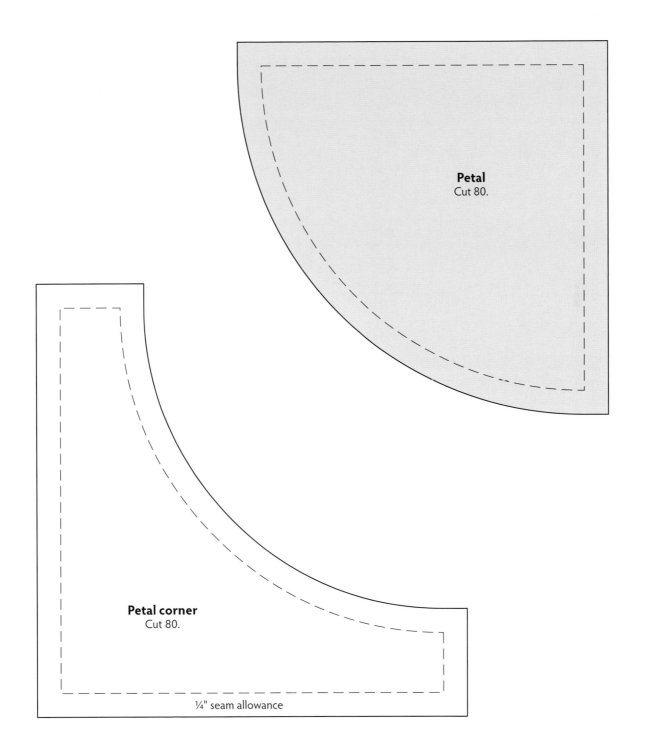

Petal
Cut 80.

Petal corner
Cut 80.

¼" seam allowance

Stylized sailboats and X shapes combine in these blocks. Crisp white sashing with red cornerstones separates the blocks.

high tide

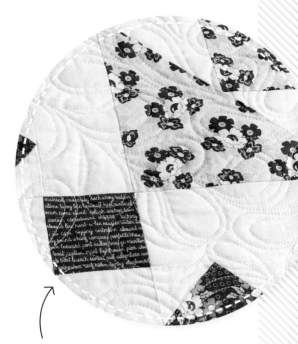

▨▨ **QUILT SIZE:** 77" × 95½"
▨▨ **BLOCK SIZE:** 16" × 16"

MATERIALS

Yardage is based on 42"-wide fabric, except as noted. Fat quarters are 18" × 21". Fat eighths are 9" × 21".

- 5⅝ yards of white solid for block backgrounds, sashing, and border
- 20 fat quarters OR 40 fat eighths of assorted prints for blocks
- ⅜ yard of cream print for X centers
- 1 yard of red print for cornerstones and binding
- 7⅛ yards of fabric for backing
- 85" × 104" piece of batting

Bonnie Says: Including cornerstones in your sashing—even if they're the same color as the longer sashing strips—helps keep all the blocks aligned in straight rows. Pressing adjoining seams in opposite directions helps them nest as well.

CUTTING

All measurements include ¼" seam allowances.

From the white solid, cut:

5 strips, 4⅜" × 42"; crosscut into 40 squares, 4⅜" × 4⅜". Cut each square into quarters diagonally to make 160 *medium* triangles.

5 strips, 4¼" × 42"; crosscut into 40 squares, 4¼" × 4¼". Cut each square in half diagonally to make 80 *large* triangles.

32 strips, 3" × 42"; crosscut into:
   31 strips, 3" × 16½"
   80 rectangles, 3" × 7¼"
   12 squares, 3" × 3"

9 strips, 3" × 42"

6 strips, 2⅝" × 42"; crosscut into 80 squares, 2⅝" × 2⅝". Cut each square in half diagonally to make 160 *small* triangles.

From the assorted prints, cut 20 *matching sets* of:

1 square, 7⅝" × 7⅝"; cut each square in half diagonally to make 2 triangles (40 total)

2 squares, 3⅞" × 3⅞" (40 total)

From the remainder of the assorted prints, cut 20 *matching sets* of:

8 rectangles, 2¾" × 3" (160 total)

From the cream print, cut:

4 strips, 3" × 42"; crosscut into 40 squares, 3" × 3"

From the red print, cut:

2 strips, 3" × 42"; crosscut into 20 squares, 3" × 3"

10 strips, 2½" × 42"

31

Designed and pieced by **BONNIE OLAVESON;** machine quilted by **LEANN POWELL**

MAKING THE BLOCKS

Sew pieces right sides together. Press all seam allowances as indicated by the arrows.

1 For one block, choose two sets of pieces from the assorted prints (eight rectangles from one print; two triangles and two squares from a contrasting print).

2 When making unit A, be sure to use a scant ¼" seam allowance. To make unit A, lay out four rectangles from the first print, four small white triangles, four medium white triangles, and one cream print square in five rows. Sew the pieces in each row; press. Join rows to make unit A, which should measure 7¼" square, including the seam allowances. Repeat to make two.

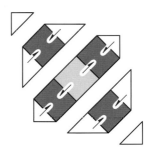

Make 2 of unit A,
7¼" × 7¼".

3 To make unit B, sew large white triangles to adjacent edges of a print square; press. Add a print triangle to the long edge of the pieced triangle to make unit B, which should measure 7¼" square, including the seam allowances; press. Repeat to make two.

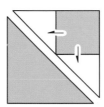
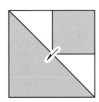

Make 2 of unit B,
7¼" × 7¼".

4 Arrange two of unit A, two of unit B, four white 3" × 7¼" sashing rectangles, and one red print 3" sashing square as shown. Stitch the pieces together in each row; press. Join the rows to make a block; press. The block should measure 16½" square, including the seam allowances. Repeat to make 20 blocks.

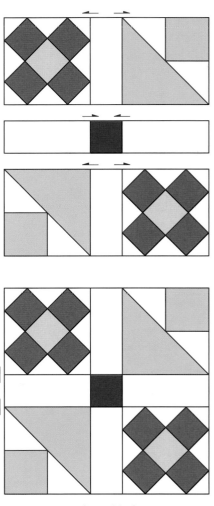

Make 20 blocks,
16½" × 16½".

Remembering Color Combinations

I like to do all of my cutting at once and then place each block in a separate pile or resealable plastic bag so that I can sew each block without mixing up my planned color combinations.

ASSEMBLING THE QUILT TOP

1 Lay out the blocks in five rows of four blocks per row, leaving space between the blocks for the white 3" × 16½" strips. Add the white strips vertically in each block row and horizontally between the block rows. Add the white 3" squares between the horizontal white strips.

2 Sew the pieces in each block row together and press. Sew the pieces in each sashing row together and press. Join the block and sashing rows to complete the quilt-top center, which should measure 72" × 90½".

3 For the border, sew the white 3"-wide strips together end to end; press the seam allowances open. Measure the width of the quilt top, which should measure 72", and cut two border strips to this length. Sew the border strips to the top and bottom edges of the quilt top. Press.

4 Measure the length of the quilt top, which should now be 95½", and cut two border strips to this length. Sew the border strips to the sides of the quilt top. Press.

FINISHING THE QUILT

For more explanation on any of the finishing steps, go to ShopMartingale.com/HowtoQuilt for free downloadable information.

1 Prepare the quilt backing so it's about 8" larger in both directions than the quilt top.

2 Layer the backing (right side down), batting, and quilt top (right side up). Baste the layers together.

3 Hand or machine quilt; the quilt shown is quilted with an allover double teardrop.

4 Use the red print 2½"-wide strips to make binding and attach it to the quilt.

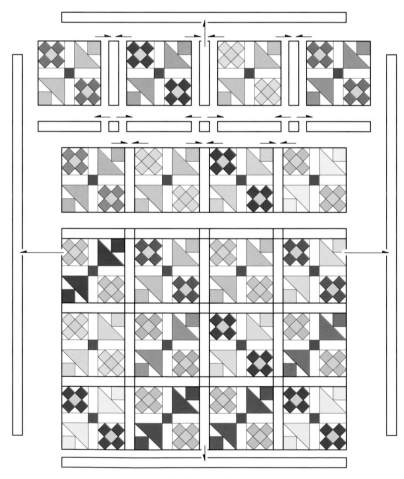

Quilt assembly

baskets of marmalade

Pinwheels make up sweet Basket blocks and are also repeated in a happy pieced border for this medallion-style throw.

QUILT SIZE: 62" × 62"
BASKET BLOCK SIZE: 7¾" × 7¾"
PINWHEEL BLOCK SIZE: 3" × 3"

MATERIALS

Yardage is based on 42"-wide fabric, except as noted.

- 36 to 42 squares, 10" × 10", of assorted prints for blocks and 2nd border
- 4 yards of white solid for block backgrounds, sashing, and 1st and 3rd borders
- ⅓ yard of pink print for 4th border
- ¾ yard of green stripe for bias binding
- 3⅞ yards of fabric for backing
- 68" × 68" piece of batting
- 1 yard of 17"-wide fusible web

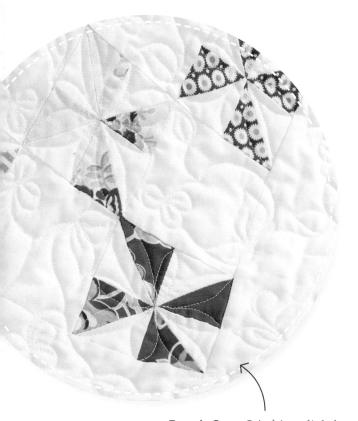

Bonnie Says: Stitching slightly oversized units and then trimming them down makes it much easier to piece the blocks accurately.

CUTTING

All measurements include ¼" seam allowances. The handles on the Basket blocks are appliquéd using fusible web. To use fusible web, trace the pattern (page 41) 16 times onto the paper side of fusible web with a pencil, leaving ½" between tracings. Cut out each fusible-web shape roughly ¼" around the drawn lines. Following the manufacturer's instructions, press the fusible web onto the wrong side of the indicated fabric, and then cut out the fabric shape on the drawn line.

From *each of 16* of the 10" squares, cut:

1 square, 4⅛" × 4⅛"; cut in half diagonally to make 2 triangles (32 total)

1 square, 2½" × 2½" (16 total)

1 handle using the pattern and fusible web (16 total)

From scraps of the 16 cut squares and the remaining 10" squares, cut:

80 *pairs* of matching squares, 2½" × 2½" (160 total)

From the white solid, cut:

2 strips, 7⅛" × 42"; crosscut into 8 squares, 7⅛" × 7⅛". Cut each square in half diagonally to make 16 triangles.

6 strips, 5" × 42"

10 strips, 3½" × 42"; crosscut into:
    16 rectangles, 3½" × 8¼"
    60 squares, 3½" × 3½"

12 strips, 2½" × 42"; crosscut into 176 squares, 2½" × 2½"

6 strips, 2" × 42"; crosscut into:
    32 rectangles, 2" × 5¼"
    16 squares, 2" × 2"

4 strips, 1½" × 42" (Don't cut until you're ready to stitch the borders in place. You may need to change the size to ensure the 2nd pieced border fits.)

From the pink print, cut:

7 strips, 1¼" × 42

From the green stripe, cut:

Enough 2½"-wide bias strips to total 270"

Designed and pieced by **BONNIE OLAVESON;** machine quilted by **LEANN POWELL**

MAKING THE BLOCKS

Sew pieces right sides together. Press all seam allowances as indicated by the arrows.

1 Using a pencil and ruler, mark a diagonal line from corner to corner on the wrong side of the white 2½" squares.

2 To make the Pinwheel blocks, gather the 80 pairs of matching 2½" squares from assorted prints. Place a marked white square on each print 2½" square in a set, right sides together, and stitch a scant ¼" from both sides of the marked diagonal lines. Cut on the marked lines and press to make four matching half-square-triangle units. Trim the units to 2" square. Repeat to make 80 sets of four matching half-square-triangle units (320 total).

Make 320
(80 sets of 4),
2" × 2".

3 Lay out a set of four matching half-square-triangle units in two rows. Sew the pieces in each row together and press. Matching the center seams, stitch the two rows together to make a Pinwheel block; press. The block should measure 3½" square, including the seam allowances; make sure you trim all sides of the block equally so that the pinwheel is centered. Repeat to make 80 Pinwheel blocks.

Make 80 blocks,
3½" x 3½".

4 To make the Basket blocks, gather pieces from one assorted print (two triangles, one 2½" square, and one handle) and a Pinwheel block from a different print. Stitch the triangles to two adjacent edges of the Pinwheel block; press.

 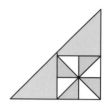

5 Peel the paper backing off of the handle and fold it in half to mark the center; unfold. Fold a white triangle in half to mark the center; unfold. Matching center creases and aligning the ends of the handle with the bottom of the triangle, fuse the handle to the triangle. Sew around the curved edges of the handle using a machine zigzag or blanket stitch. I used white thread to blanket-stitch all of the handles in the quilt shown.

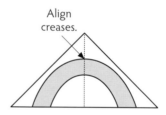

Align creases.

6 Stitch the handle triangle to the unit from step 4 to make a basket unit; press. The basket unit should measure 6¾" square, including the seam allowances.

Make 16 units,
6¾" × 6¾".

7 Place a remaining marked white 2½" square on the print 2½" square, right sides together, and stitch a scant ¼" from both sides of the marked diagonal line. Cut on the marked line and press to make two matching half-square-triangle units. Trim each unit to 2" square, including seam allowances.

Make 2.

8 Position two white 2" × 5¼" rectangles, the two half-square-triangle units, and one white 2" square along adjacent edges of the basket unit as shown. Stitch the pieces into rows; press. Sew the rows to the sides of the basket unit; press to make a Basket block, which should measure 8¼" square, including the seam allowances. Make 16 Basket blocks.

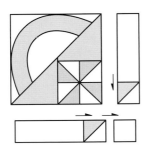

Make 16 blocks,
8¼" × 8¼".

9 Arrange four Basket blocks, four white 3½" × 8¼" strips, and one Pinwheel block in three rows as shown. Stitch the pieces together in each row; press. Join the rows to make a four-block section,

which should measure 19" square, including the seam allowances. Repeat to make four sections.

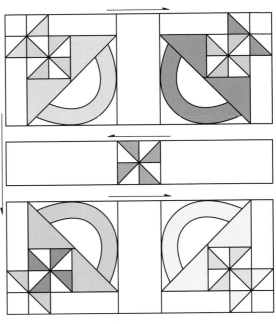

Make 4 sections,
19" × 19".

ASSEMBLING THE QUILT TOP

1 Lay out the four-block sections in two rows of two sections each. Sew the sections in each row together and press the seams in opposite directions. Join the rows to complete the quilt-top center, which should measure 37½" square.

2 To match the length of the second border, which is pieced, the quilt center needs to measure 39½" square after the first border is added. If your quilt measures exactly 37½" square right now, cut the white inner-border strips 1½" wide. If your quilt is smaller than this, adjust accordingly by cutting the border strips wider; if your quilt is larger than this, cut the border strips narrower. Measure the width of the quilt top and cut two border strips to this length. Sew the border strips to the sides of the quilt top. Measure the length of the quilt top and cut two border strips to this length. Sew the border strips to the top and bottom of the quilt. Press.

3 To make the second border, lay out 13 Pinwheel blocks and 13 white 3½" squares as shown. Sew the pieces together into rows; press. Join the rows. Make two. Sew the borders to the sides of the quilt top; press.

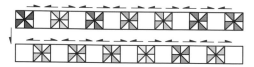

Make 2 side borders,
6½" × 39½".

4 Lay out 17 Pinwheel blocks and 17 white 3½" squares as shown. Sew the pieces together into rows; press. Join the rows. Make two. Sew the borders to the top and bottom of quilt top; press.

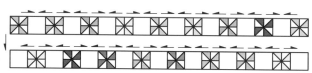

Make 2 top and bottom borders,
6½" × 51½".

5 For the third border, sew the white 5"-wide strips together end to end and press the seam allowances open. Measure the width of the quilt top, which should be 51½", and cut two border strips to this length. Sew the border strips to opposite edges of the quilt top. Measure the length of the quilt top, which should be 60½", and cut two border strips to this length. Sew the border strips to the top and bottom of the quilt. Press. (To make sure the fourth border is as straight as possible—because it's a skinny border being added to a wider third border—it will be added after the quilt top is quilted.)

Quilt assembly

FINISHING THE QUILT

For more explanation on any of the finishing steps, go to ShopMartingale.com/HowtoQuilt for free downloadable information.

1. Prepare the quilt backing so it's about 6" larger in both directions than the quilt top.

2. Layer the backing (right side down), batting, and quilt top (right side up). Baste the layers together.

3. Hand or machine quilt. *Don't trim the backing and batting away yet.* The quilt shown is quilted with curved lines in each assorted print piece and an allover design of leaves and flowers in the white background.

4. To add the fourth border, sew the pink 1¼"-wide strips together end to end; press the seam allowances open. Measure the width of the quilt top, which should be 60½", and cut two border strips to this length. Sew the border strips to opposite edges of the quilt top, stitching through the quilt top, batting, and backing. Press the strips open, pressing the seam allowances toward the pink borders. Measure the length of the quilt top, which should now be 62", and cut two border strips to this length. Sew the border strips to the top and bottom of the quilt top, stitching through the quilt top, batting, and backing. Press the seam allowances toward the pink borders. Trim the backing and batting even with the quilt-top edge.

5. Use the green stripe 2½"-wide strips to make binding and attach it to the quilt.

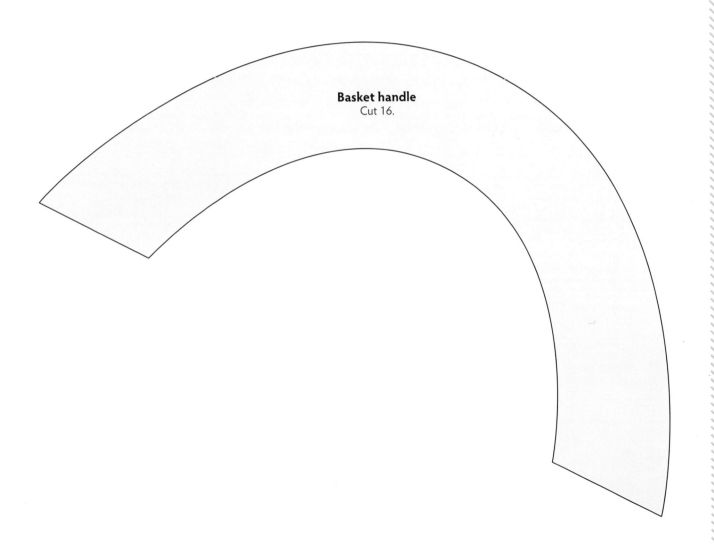

Basket handle
Cut 16.

modern
vintage

Feed sack–inspired fabrics look fresh and fun on a crisp white background in this Crown of Thorns quilt. The block is also known as the Single Wedding Ring.

QUILT SIZE: 70½" × 70½"
BLOCK SIZE: 10" × 10"

MATERIALS

Yardage is based on 42"-wide fabric, except as noted.

- 4¼ yards of white solid for block backgrounds
- 63 squares, 10" × 10", of assorted prints for blocks (15 green, 15 red, 8 mint, 8 navy, 8 aqua, 5 pink, and 4 orange)
- ⅝ yard of red diagonal stripe for binding
- 4⅓ yards of fabric for backing
- 77" × 77" piece of batting

CUTTING

All measurements include ¼" seam allowances.

From the white solid, cut:

31 strips, 3" × 42"; crosscut into 392 squares, 3" × 3"

17 strips, 2½" × 42"; crosscut into 245 squares, 2½" × 2½"

From *each of 49* of the 10" squares (12 green, 12 red, 6 mint, 6 navy, 6 aqua, 4 pink, and 3 orange), refer to cutting diagram A below to cut:

6 squares, 3" × 3" (294 total)

4 squares, 2½" × 2½" (196 total)

From *each of the 14 remaining* 10" squares (3 green, 3 red, 2 mint, 2 navy, 2 aqua, 1 pink, and 1 orange), refer to cutting diagram B to cut:

8 squares, 3" × 3" (112 total)

From the red diagonal stripe, cut:

8 strips, 2½" × 42" (To get a barber's pole look if your fabric isn't a diagonal stripe, cut your strips on the bias instead.)

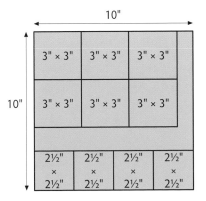

Cutting diagram A

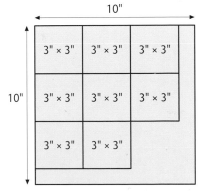

Cutting diagram B

The Right Proportions

If you're using fabrics different from those listed (or in a different proportion of colors), know that each block requires four 2½" squares and eight 3" squares in the same colorway (plus the solid white pieces). You'll need 49 total sets of pieces.

MAKING THE BLOCKS

Sew pieces right sides together. Press all seam allowances as indicated by the arrows.

1. Using a pencil and ruler, mark a diagonal line from corner to corner on the wrong side of each white 3" square.

2. Place a marked white square on a print 3" square, right sides together, and stitch ¼" from both sides of the marked line. Cut on the marked line and press to make two matching half-square-triangle units. Trim the units to 2½" square, including the seam allowances.

3. Repeat step 2 to make the following number and color of half-square-triangle units. You'll have some extra squares of mint, navy, aqua, and orange left over. (If you're using colors different from those listed, construct a total of 784 half-square-triangle units—49 sets of 16 matching units.)

Make 192 each.   Make 96 each.

Make 64.   Make 48.

4. Lay out 16 same-color half-square-triangle units, four same-color print 2½" squares, and five white 2½" squares in five horizontal rows as shown. Stitch the pieces in each row. Press. Join the rows to make a Crown of Thorns block. The block should measure 10½" square, including the seam allowances. Repeat to make 49 blocks (12 green, 12 red, 6 mint, 6 navy, 6 aqua, 4 pink, and 3 orange).

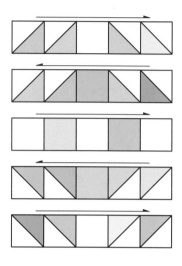

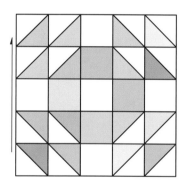

Make 49 blocks,
10½" × 10½".

Cooperating Colors

Combining two or three fabric lines that play nicely together gives a scrappy quilt more of an intentional look. My granddaughter, Livvy, helped me piece this one out of Hello Darling and Daysail fabric by Bonnie and Camille for Moda Fabrics.

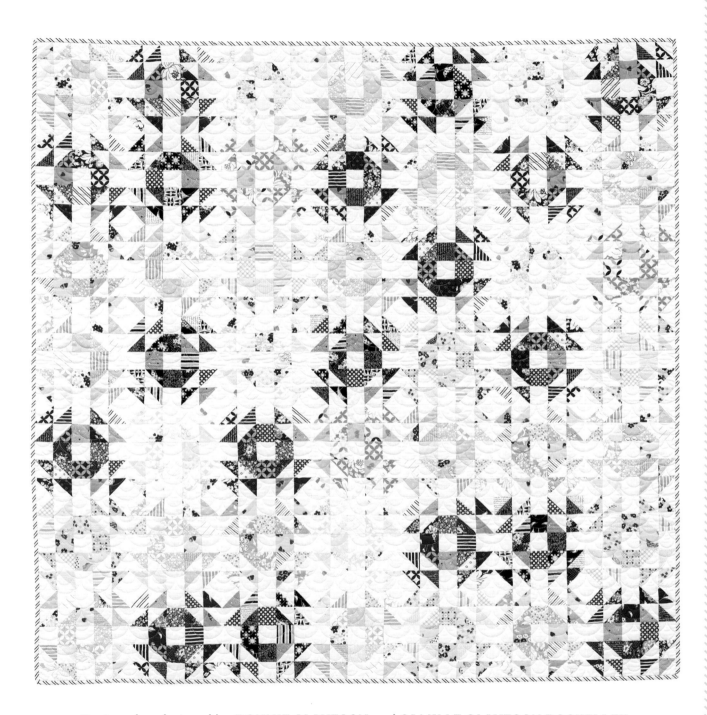

Designed and pieced by **BONNIE OLAVESON** and **CAMILLE OLAVESON ROSKELLEY**;
machine quilted by **ABBY LATIMER**

ASSEMBLING THE QUILT TOP

Lay out the blocks in seven rows of seven blocks per row. Rotate every other block 90° so the seams nest. Sew the blocks in each row together and press. Join the block rows to complete the quilt top, which should measure 70½" × 70½".

FINISHING THE QUILT

For more explanation on any of the finishing steps, go to ShopMartingale.com/HowtoQuilt for free downloadable information.

1 Prepare the quilt backing so it's about 6" larger in both directions than the quilt top.

2 Layer the backing (right side down), batting, and quilt top (right side up). Baste the layers together.

3 Hand or machine quilt; the quilt shown is quilted with a double clamshell pattern.

4 Use the red diagonal stripe 2½"-wide strips to make binding and attach it to the quilt.

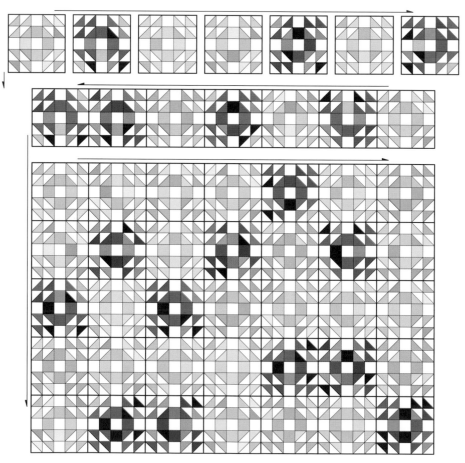

Quilt assembly

cabin christmas

Bring tradition home for the holidays with classic Log Cabin blocks—then add some modern flair with Flower blocks shaped like poinsettias.

 **QUILT SIZE:** 72½" × 72½"
BLOCK SIZE: 12" × 12"

MATERIALS

Yardage is based on 42"-wide fabric.

- 3⅓ yards of cream dot for blocks
- ¼ yard of red print for Log Cabin blocks
- ⅜ yard of green diagonal stripe for Log Cabin blocks
- ⅝ yard of green dot for Log Cabin blocks
- 1 yard of green print for blocks
- 1½ yards of red dot for Flower blocks
- ⅝ yard of red diagonal stripe for binding
- 4½ yards of fabric for backing
- 79" × 79" piece of batting

> **Bonnie Says:** Don't be afraid to use a holiday pattern like this one in a totally different colorway. Think Fourth of July, fall, or red and pink for Valentine's Day. You could even make it totally scrappy. Be creative and give it your own look!

CUTTING

All measurements include ¼" seam allowances.

From the cream dot, cut:

4 strips, 3⅝" × 42"; crosscut into 36 squares, 3⅝" × 3⅝". Cut each square into quarters diagonally to make 144 *small* triangles.

11 strips, 3" × 42"; crosscut into 72 rectangles, 3" × 5¼"

6 strips, 2⅞" × 42"; crosscut into 72 squares, 2⅞" × 2⅞"

21 strips, 2" × 42"; crosscut into:
   18 K strips, 2" × 11"
   18 J strips, 2" × 9½"
   18 G strips, 2" × 8"
   18 F strips, 2" × 6½"
   18 C strips, 2" × 5"
   18 B strips, 2" × 3½"

From the red print, cut:

2 strips, 3½" × 42"; crosscut into 18 A squares, 3½" × 3½"

From the green diagonal stripe, cut:

6 strips, 2" × 42"; crosscut into:
   18 E strips, 2" × 6½"
   18 D strips, 2" × 5"

From the green dot, cut:

9 strips, 2" × 42"; crosscut into:
   18 I strips, 2" × 9½"
   18 H strips, 2" × 8"

From the green print, cut:

2 strips, 3" × 42"; crosscut into 18 squares, 3" × 3"

12 strips, 2" × 42"; crosscut into:
   18 M strips, 2" × 12½"
   18 L strips, 2" × 11"

From the red dot, cut:

6 strips, 5⅝" × 42"; crosscut into 36 squares, 5⅝" × 5⅝". Cut each square in half diagonally to make 72 *large* triangles.

4 strips, 3⅝" × 42"; crosscut into 36 squares, 3⅝" × 3⅝". Cut each square into quarters diagonally to make 144 *small* triangles.

From the red diagonal stripe, cut:

8 strips, 2½" × 42"

Designed and pieced by **BONNIE OLAVESON**; machine quilted by **LEANN POWELL**

MAKING THE LOG CABIN BLOCKS

Sew pieces right sides together. Press all seam allowances as indicated by the arrows. Add all the strips in a counterclockwise direction.

Stitch a cream B strip to the top of a red A square; press. Add a cream C strip to the left edge of the square. Then stitch green D and E strips to the remaining edges to complete the first round of piecing. Working in alphabetical order, continue adding strips, pressing after each addition, to make a Log Cabin block. The block should measure 12½" square, including the seam allowances. Make 18 Log Cabin blocks.

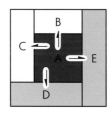

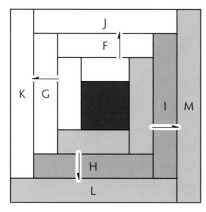

Make 18 blocks,
12½" × 12½".

MAKING THE FLOWER BLOCKS

1 Join small red and cream triangles as shown; make 72 triangle pairs where the red triangle is on the left (unit A) and 72 where the red triangle is on the right (unit B). Press.

Make 72 of   Make 72 of
triangle pair A.   triangle pair B.

2 Sew a unit A and a unit B to adjacent edges of a cream 2⅞" square; press. Add a large red triangle to the long edge to make a petal unit, which should measure 5¼" square, including the seam allowances. Repeat to make 72 petal units.

Make 72 units,
5¼" × 5¼".

3 Lay out four petal units, four cream 3" × 5¼" rectangles, and one green 3" square in three rows as shown. Join the pieces in each row; press. Join the rows to make a Flower block; press. The block should measure 12½" square, including the seam allowances. Make 18 Flower blocks.

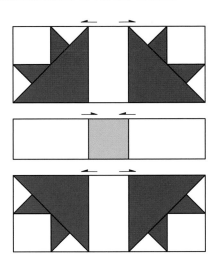

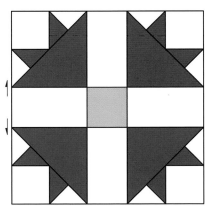

Make 18 blocks,
12½" × 12½".

ASSEMBLING THE QUILT TOP

1 Lay out the blocks in six rows of six blocks per row, alternating between Log Cabin and Flower blocks and orienting the Log Cabin blocks as shown below.

2 Sew the blocks in each row together. Press. Join the block rows to complete the quilt top, which should measure 72½" × 72½".

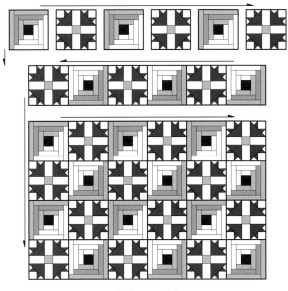

Quilt assembly

FINISHING THE QUILT

For more explanation on any of the finishing steps, go to ShopMartingale.com/HowtoQuilt for free downloadable information.

1 Prepare the quilt backing so it's about 6" larger in both directions than the quilt top.

2 Layer the backing (right side down), batting, and quilt top (right side up). Baste the layers together.

3 Hand or machine quilt; the quilt shown is quilted with an allover spiral design interspersed with ribbon candy motifs and poinsettias.

4 Use the red diagonal stripe 2½"-wide strips to make binding and attach it to the quilt.

Start with a square-in-a-square unit and cleverly add to it to create adorable Butterfly blocks.

all aflutter

 QUILT SIZE: 65½" × 79½"
BLOCK SIZE: 12" × 12"

MATERIALS

Yardage is based on 42"-wide fabric, except as noted.

- 4 yards of white solid for block backgrounds, inner border, and outer border
- 40 squares, 10" × 10" *each,* of assorted prints for blocks (perfect for a Layer Cake!)
- ½ yard of red print for middle border
- ⅝ yard of aqua print for binding
- 4⅞ yards of fabric for backing
- 72" × 86" piece of batting

CUTTING

All measurements include ¼" seam allowances.

From the white solid, cut:

6 strips, 4½" × 42"; crosscut into 80 rectangles, 2½" × 4½"

4 strips, 3¾" × 42"; crosscut into 40 squares, 3¾" × 3¾". Cut each square in half diagonally to make 80 triangles.

7 strips, 2⅞" × 42"; crosscut into 80 squares, 2⅞" × 2⅞"

12 strips, 2½" × 42"; crosscut into:
31 strips, 2½" × 12½"
12 squares, 2½" × 2½"

15 strips, 2½" × 42"

From *each of 20* of the 10" squares, refer to the cutting diagram below to cut:

1 square, 4⅞" × 4⅞"; cut each square in half diagonally to make 40 triangles

1 square, 4½" × 4½" (20 total)

2 squares, 2⅞" × 2⅞" (40 total)

2 squares, 2½" × 2½" (40 total)

From *each of the 20 remaining* 10" squares, cut:

1 square, 4⅞" × 4⅞"; cut each square in half diagonally to make 40 triangles

2 squares, 2⅞" × 2⅞" (40 total)

2 squares, 2½" × 2½" (40 total)

From the red print, cut:

7 strips, 2" × 42"

From the aqua print, cut:

8 strips, 2½" × 42"

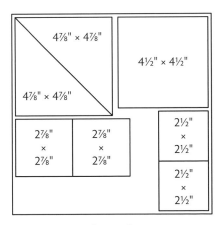

Cutting from 10" squares

Designed and pieced by **BONNIE OLAVESON;** machine quilted by **LEANN POWELL**

MAKING THE BLOCKS

Sew pieces right sides together. Press all seam allowances as indicated by the arrows.

1 Using a pencil and ruler, mark a diagonal line from corner to corner on the wrong side of each white 2⅞" square.

2 Place a marked white square on a print 2⅞" square, right sides together, and stitch ¼" from each side of the marked line. Cut on the marked line and press to make two half-square-triangle units that measure 2½" square, including seam allowances. Repeat to make 160 half-square-triangle units (80 pairs of matching units).

Make 160 units,
2½" × 2½".

3 Stitch white triangles to opposite edges of a print 4½" square; press. Stitch white triangles to the remaining edges of the square to make a block center; press. The block center should measure 6¼" square, including the seam allowances. Repeat to make 20 block centers.

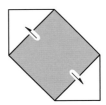 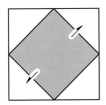

Make 20 units,
6¼" × 6¼".

4 For one block, choose a block center and four different sets of matching pieces (two half-square-triangle units, one triangle, and one 2½" square all from the same print). Stitch triangles to opposite edges of the block center as shown; press. Stitch the remaining triangles to the remaining edges of the block center; press. The block center should now be 8½" square, including the seam allowances.

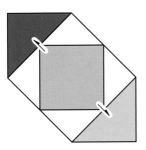

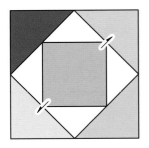

Make 20 units,
8½" × 8½".

Distributing Colors

For each block, you'll need to choose four different fabrics for the corners (each corner needs one triangle, one 2⅞" square, and one 2½" square of the same fabric) and a fifth fabric for the center 4½" square. I suggest separating your cut fabric into blocks before starting to stitch so the colors are well distributed throughout the quilt. You may even want to put them in little bags and stitch just one block at a time.

5 Arrange the pieced block center with the remaining print pieces and white rectangles as shown. Stitch the half-square-triangle units to the white rectangles; press. Then sew the pieces in three horizontal rows; press. Join the rows to make a block; press. The block should measure 12½" square, including the seam allowances. Make 20 blocks.

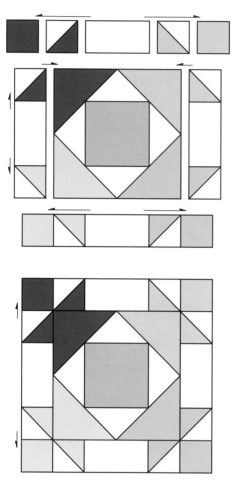

Make 20 blocks,
12½" × 12½".

ASSEMBLING THE QUILT TOP

1 Lay out the blocks in five rows of four blocks per row, leaving space between the blocks for the white 2½" × 12½" strips. Add the white strips vertically in each block row and horizontally between the block rows. Lay out the white 2½" squares between the horizontal white strips.

2 Sew the pieces in each block row together and press. Sew the pieces in each sashing row together and press. Join the block and sashing rows to complete the quilt-top center, which should measure 54½" × 68½".

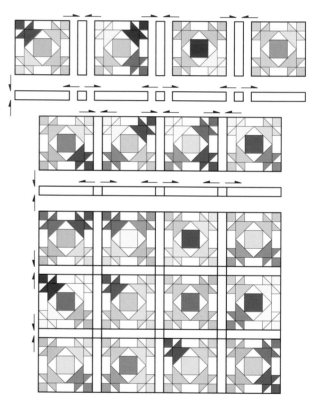

Quilt assembly

3 For the inner border, sew seven white 2½"-wide strips together end to end; press the seam allowances open. Measure the width of the quilt top, which should be 54½", and cut two border strips to this length. Sew the border strips to the top and bottom edges of the quilt top. Press.

Why Piece the Sashing?

Although you could cut long sashing strips instead of piecing the horizontal white sashing rectangles and cornerstones, piecing is an easy way to ensure perfect placement when joining rows. Because you're aligning seams as you go, your blocks and sashing pieces will all line up.

4 Measure the length of the quilt top, which should be 72½", and cut two border strips to this length. Sew the border strips to the sides of the quilt top. Press the seam allowances toward the white borders.

5 For the middle border, repeat steps 3 and 4 using the red 2"-wide strips. Press.

6 For the outer border, repeat steps 3 and 4 using the remaining white 2½"-wide strips. Press.

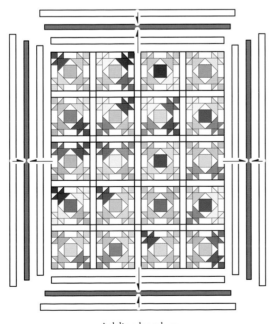

Adding borders

FINISHING THE QUILT

For more explanation on any of the finishing steps, go to ShopMartingale.com/HowtoQuilt for free downloadable information.

1 Prepare the quilt backing so it's about 6" larger in both directions than the quilt top.

2 Layer the backing (right side down), batting, and quilt top (right side up). Baste the layers together.

3 Hand or machine quilt; the quilt shown is quilted with an allover swirl design.

4 Use the aqua 2½"-wide strips to make binding and attach it to the quilt.

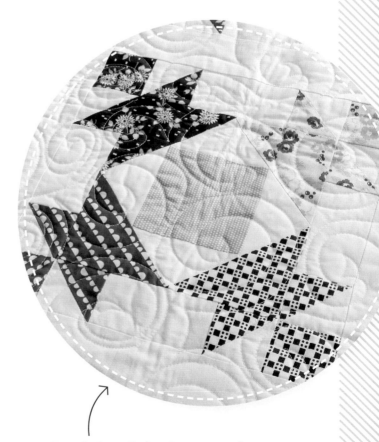

Bonnie Says: Before I cut out and start sewing the whole quilt, I love to make one block to test it and get familiar with the piecing method. Once you're familiar with the quilt, you can chain piece with confidence. And that can be a huge time saver.

peppermint pizzazz

Indulge your sweet tooth without any calories in this holiday quilt that's just as fun for year-round use.

QUILT SIZE: 43" × 43"
PEPPERMINT BLOCK SIZE: 8" × 8"
CANDY STICK BLOCK SIZE: 5¾" × 5"
STAR BLOCK SIZE: 8" × 8"

MATERIALS

Yardage is based on 42"-wide fabric, except as noted. Fat eighths are 9" × 21".

- 1 yard of cream dot for Peppermint and Star blocks
- 1 yard of aqua dot for Peppermint blocks, sashing, and borders
- ⅓ yard of red print for Peppermint blocks
- ½ yard of green dot for Peppermint and Candy Stick blocks
- ⅝ yard of red dot for Candy Stick blocks
- ⅛ yard of pink dot for Candy Stick blocks
- ⅜ yard of aqua swirl for Candy Stick blocks
- 5 fat eighths of assorted prints for Star blocks
- ½ yard of red stripe for binding
- 2¾ yards of fabric for backing
- 49" × 49" piece of batting

CUTTING

All measurements include ¼" seam allowances.

From the cream dot, cut:

3 strips, 5" × 42"; crosscut into 20 squares, 5" × 5"

1 strip, 3¼" × 42"; crosscut into 5 squares, 3¼" × 3¼". Cut each square into quarters diagonally to make 20 *small* triangles.

1 strip, 2⅞" × 42"; crosscut into 10 squares, 2⅞" × 2⅞". Cut each square in half diagonally to make 20 *medium* triangles.

4 strips, 2½" × 42"; crosscut into:
20 rectangles, 2½" × 4½"
20 squares, 2½" × 2½"

From the aqua dot, cut:

4 strips, 3" × 42"; crosscut into 40 squares, 3" × 3"

4 strips, 2" × 40½"

2 strips, 1¾" × 40½"

3 strips, 1¾" × 42"

From the red print, cut:

2 strips, 5" × 42"; crosscut into 10 squares, 5" × 5"

From the green dot, cut:

2 strips, 5" × 42"; crosscut into 10 squares, 5" × 5"

4 strips, 1½" × 42"

From the red dot, cut:

2 strips, 5½" × 42"; crosscut into 56 rectangles, ¾" × 5½"

4 strips, 1½" × 42"

From the pink dot, cut:

2 strips, 1½" × 42"

From the aqua swirl, cut:

2 strips, 5½" × 42"; crosscut into 42 rectangles, 1¼" × 5½"

From *each* assorted print, cut:

1 square, 3¼" × 3¼"; cut each square into quarters diagonally to make 20 *small* triangles

8 squares, 2½" × 2½" (40 total)

From the red stripe, cut:

5 strips, 2½" × 42"

Designed and pieced by **BONNIE OLAVESON;** machine quilted by **LEANN POWELL**

MAKING THE PEPPERMINT BLOCKS

Sew pieces right sides together. Press all seam allowances as indicated by the arrows.

1 Using a pencil and ruler, mark a diagonal line from corner to corner on the wrong side of each cream 5" square and aqua dot 3" square. Set the aqua squares aside for now.

2 Place a marked cream square on a red print 5" square, right sides together, and stitch ¼" from both sides of the marked line. Cut on the marked line and press to make two half-square-triangle units. Trim each unit to 4½" square, including the seam allowances. Repeat to make 20 red half-square-triangle units. Repeat using green dot squares instead of red print to make 20 green units.

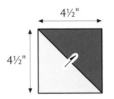

4½"

4½"

Make 20 red units and
20 green units.

3 Sew together four red half-square-triangle units in two rows as shown; press. Join the rows to make a pinwheel unit. Repeat to make five red pinwheel units and five green pinwheel units.

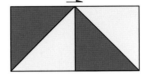

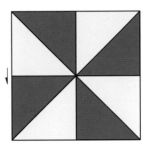

Make 5 red and 5 green units,
8½" × 8½".

Bonnie Says: Adding aqua to the traditional red and green Christmas colors can give your holiday quilts a fresh look. For the quilting, swirls were stitched in the peppermints to create motion.

4 Place a marked aqua square on one corner of a pinwheel unit, right sides together, and stitch on the marked line. Trim the excess corner fabric, leaving a ¼" seam allowance. Press. Repeat, sewing an aqua square to each corner to make a Peppermint block, which should measure 8½" square, including the seam allowances. Repeat to make five red Peppermint blocks and five green Peppermint blocks.

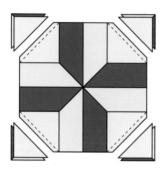

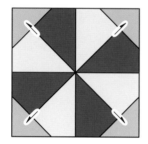

Make 5 red and 5 green blocks,
8½" × 8½".

Picture Your Motifs

When choosing fabrics for a quilt with prominent motifs like the stars and peppermints in this design, I lay out my fabrics and take a picture in black and white. The gray tones of the photo show relative values without the distraction of color, revealing whether the fabric for the main motif will stand out from the rest.

MAKING THE CANDY STICK BLOCKS

1 Aligning the long edges, sew together one pink dot, two red dot, and two green dot 1½" × 42" strips as shown. Press the seam allowances in one direction. The strip set should measure 5½" × 42", including the seam allowances. Repeat to make a second strip set. Trim each strip set at a 45° angle. Cutting parallel to the angled edge, cut 28 candy stick segments, each 1¾" wide.

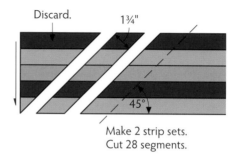

Discard.   1¾"

45°

Make 2 strip sets.
Cut 28 segments.

2 Trim each segment to 5½" tall.

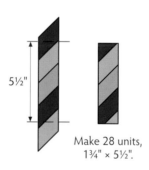

5½"

Make 28 units,
1¾" × 5½".

3 Stitch red dot ¾" × 5½" rectangles to both long edges of each candy stick; press. Then join two candy sticks and three aqua swirl 1¼" × 5½" rectangles to make a Candy Stick block; press. The block should measure 6¼" × 5½", including the seam allowances. Make 14 Candy Stick blocks.

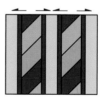

Make 28 units,   Make 14 blocks,
2¼" × 5½".   5½" × 6¼".

MAKING THE STAR BLOCKS

1. For one Star block, gather eight 2½" squares from one of the assorted prints for the star points and four triangles from a different print for the pinwheel center.

2. Stitch together a print triangle and a small cream triangle with the print triangle on the left; press. Add a medium cream triangle to the long edges to make a triangle unit, which should measure 2½" square, including the seam allowances; press. Repeat to make four triangle units.

Make 4 units,
2½" × 2½".

3. Sew together four triangle units in two rows as shown; press. Join rows to make a small pinwheel unit, which should measure 4½" square, including the seam allowances. Press.

Make 1 unit,
4½" × 4½".

4. Using a pencil and ruler, mark a diagonal line from corner to corner on the wrong side of the eight print 2½" squares. Place a marked square on one end of a cream 2½" × 4½" rectangle, right sides together, and stitch on the marked line. Trim the excess corner fabric, leaving a ¼" seam allowance. Press. Add another marked square to the other end of the cream rectangle, making sure the diagonal line is facing the correct direction to make a flying-geese unit. Press. Repeat to make four matching flying-geese units.

 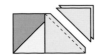

Make 4 units,
2½" × 4½".

5. Lay out the four flying-geese units, the small pinwheel unit, and four cream 2½" squares in three rows as shown. Sew the pieces in each row; press. Join the rows to make a Star block; press. The block should measure 8½" square, including the seam allowances. Make five Star blocks.

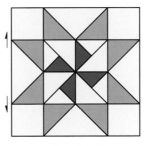

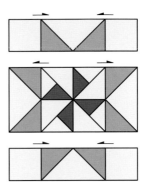

Make 5 blocks,
8½" × 8½".

ASSEMBLING THE QUILT TOP

Refer to the quilt assembly diagram on page 64 for all steps.

1. For the quilt's top row, sew together three red and two green Peppermint blocks, alternating colors. Press. The row should measure 8½" × 40½", including the seam allowances. Using three green Peppermint blocks and two red Peppermint blocks, make the bottom row.

2. Stitch seven Candy Stick blocks together to make the quilt's second row. Press. If necessary, trim the row to 5½" × 40½", including the seam allowances; trim even amounts off both ends of the row. Repeat to make another for the quilt's fourth row.

③ Rotating every other block so the seams nest, join five Star blocks to make the quilt's middle row. Press. The row should measure 8½" × 40½", including the seam allowances.

④ Join the aqua dot 2" × 40½" strips between the rows to make the quilt center as shown. The quilt center should measure 40½" square, including the seam allowances. Press.

⑤ Sew the aqua dot 1¾" × 40½" strips to the top and bottom edges of the quilt top. Press.

⑥ Sew together the aqua dot 1¾" × 42" strips end to end and press the seam allowances open. Measure the length of the quilt top, which should now be 43", and cut two strips this long. Sew the strips to the sides of the quilt top. Press.

FINISHING THE QUILT

For more explanation on any of the finishing steps, go to ShopMartingale.com/HowtoQuilt for free downloadable information.

① Prepare the quilt backing so it's about 6" larger in both directions than the quilt top.

② Layer the backing (right side down), batting, and quilt top (right side up). Baste the layers together.

③ Hand or machine quilt; each Peppermint block in the quilt shown is quilted with a spiral, while the remainder of the quilt is quilted with a swirl and loop design.

④ Use the red stripe 2½"-wide strips to make binding and attach it to the quilt.

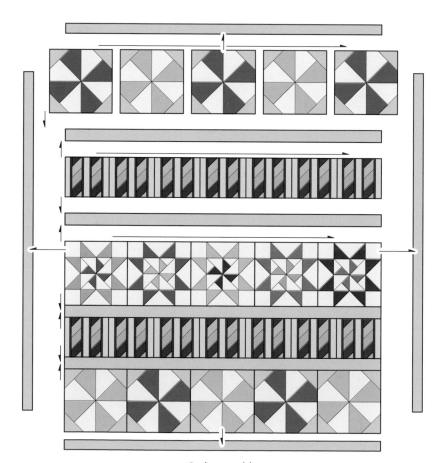

Quilt assembly

wish

No tricky curved piecing here! You can use fusible appliqué or soft raw-edge appliqué for an easy quilt with big impact.

QUILT SIZE: 49½" × 58"
BLOCK SIZE: 8½" × 8½"

MATERIALS

Yardage is based on 42"-wide fabric, except as noted.

- 20 squares, 10" × 10", of assorted prints for blocks
- 1⅞ yards of white solid for block backgrounds and 1st border
- ⅞ yard of red print for 2nd border, 4th border, and binding
- 1⅛ yards of aqua print for 3rd and 5th borders
- 3⅛ yards of fabric for backing
- 56" × 64" piece of batting
- 3¾ yards of 17"-wide fusible web (optional)
- Lightweight template plastic (optional)
- Fabric marker (optional)

CUTTING

All measurements include ¼" seam allowances. The appliqué shapes will be cut in step 1 of "Making the Blocks" below.

From the white solid, cut:
10 strips, 4¾" × 42"; crosscut into 80 squares, 4¾" × 4¾"

5 strips, 2" × 42"

From the red print, cut:
6 strips, 2½" × 42"

10 strips, 1" × 42"

From the aqua print, cut:
11 strips, 3" × 42"

MAKING THE BLOCKS

Sew pieces right sides together. Press all seam allowances as indicated by the arrows.

1 Decide if you'd like to do raw-edge or fusible appliqué, and then use the directions that follow for cutting out and preparing your appliqués for your preferred method. You'll need to cut four

quarter-circle shapes from each assorted print 10" square (80 total). The quarter-circle pattern is on page 69.

For raw-edge appliqué, cut out the pieces by using a plastic template. Trace the quarter-circle pattern onto lightweight template plastic with a permanent marker and cut it out carefully on the solid lines. To use the template, lay it right side down on the wrong side of the indicated fabric and trace around it with a fabric marker; cut out the fabric shape on the drawn line.

For fusible appliqué, trace the quarter-circle pattern 80 times onto the paper side of fusible web with a pencil, leaving ½" between shapes. Cut out each fusible-web shape roughly ¼" outside the drawn lines. Following the manufacturer's instructions, press the fusible web onto the wrong side of the indicated fabric; cut out the fabric shape on the drawn line.

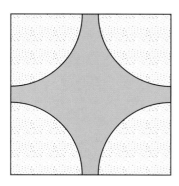

Cut 4 quarter circles
from each 10" square.

2 Position a quarter-circle shape on a white 4¾" square. **For raw-edge appliqué,** use a very small stitch to sew ⅜" from the raw curved edge. **For fusible appliqué,** remove the backing paper and fuse in place following the manufacturer's instructions. Machine blanket-stitch around the curved edge. Make 80 quarter-circle units (20 sets of four matching units).

Make 80 units,
4¾" × 4¾".

Designed and pieced by **BONNIE OLAVESON;** machine quilted by **SUSAN HANSEN**

3 Lay out four matching quarter-circle units in two rows, making sure the curve of each unit is in the proper place as shown. Sew the pieces in each row; press. Join the rows to make a block, which should measure 9" square, including the seam allowances; press. Make 20 blocks.

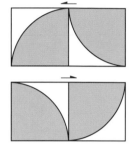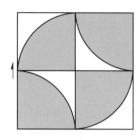

Make 20 blocks,
9" × 9".

ASSEMBLING THE QUILT TOP

1 Lay out the blocks in five rows of four blocks per row. Sew the blocks in each row together. Press. Join the rows to complete the quilt-top center, which should measure 34½" × 43".

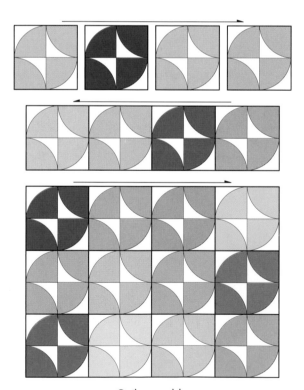

Quilt assembly

2 For the first border, measure the width of the quilt top, which should be 34½", and cut two white 2"-wide strips to this length. Sew the border strips to the top and bottom edges of the quilt top. Press.

3 Sew the three remaining white 2"-wide strips together end to end; press the seam allowances open. Measure the length of the quilt top, which should now be 46", and cut two border strips to this length. Sew the border strips to the sides of the quilt top. Press.

4 For the second border, measure the width of the quilt top, which should now be 37½", and cut two red 1"-wide strips to this length. Sew the border strips to the top and bottom edges of the quilt top. Press.

5 Sew three red 1"-wide strips together end to end; press the seam allowances open. Measure the length of the quilt top, which should now be 47", and cut two border strips to this length. Sew the border strips to the sides of the quilt top. Press.

6 For the third border, measure the width of the quilt top, which should now be 38½", and cut two aqua 3"-wide strips to this length. Sew the border strips to the top and bottom edges of the quilt top. Press.

7 Sew three aqua 3"-wide strips together end to end; press the seam allowances open. Measure the length of the quilt top, which should now be 52", and cut two border strips to this length. Sew the border strips to the sides of the quilt top. Press.

8 For the fourth border, join all the remaining red 1"-wide strips and repeat steps 4 and 5. The top and bottom borders should be 43½" long and the side borders should be 53" long.

9 For the fifth border, join all the remaining aqua 3"-wide strips and repeat steps 6 and 7. The top and bottom borders should be 44½" long and the side borders should be 58" long. The quilt top should measure 49½" × 58".

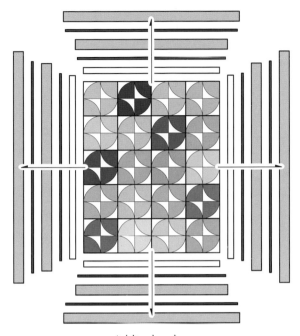

Adding borders

FINISHING THE QUILT

For more explanation on any of the finishing steps, go to ShopMartingale.com/HowtoQuilt for free downloadable information.

1 Prepare the quilt backing so it's about 6" larger in both directions than the quilt top.

2 Layer the backing (right side down), batting, and quilt top (right side up). Baste the layers together.

3 Hand or machine quilt; the quilt shown is quilted with an overall circle and loop design.

4 Use the red 2½"-wide strips to make binding and attach it to the quilt.

5 If you chose the raw-edge appliqué method, wash and dry your quilt, and then clip any stray threads.

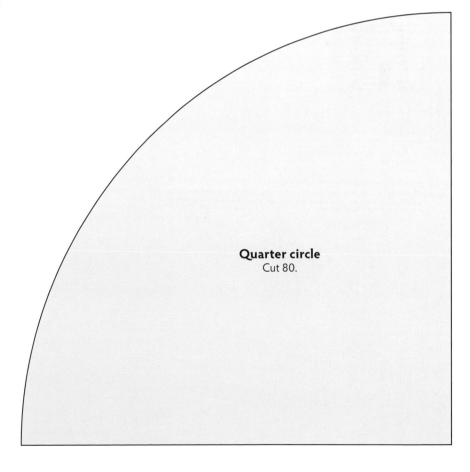

Quarter circle
Cut 80.

Supersized pinwheels spin among scrappy rectangles in a cheerful, quick-to-make throw.

sweet talk

QUILT SIZE: 76½" × 92½"
BLOCK SIZE: 16" × 16"

MATERIALS

Yardage is based on 42"-wide fabric, except as noted.

- 40 squares, 10" × 10", of assorted prints for blocks
- 2⅝ yards of red print for blocks, middle border, and binding
- 1½ yards of white print for block backgrounds
- 1⅝ yards of white solid for inner and outer borders
- 7⅛ yards of fabric for backing
- 85" × 101" piece of batting

CUTTING

All measurements include ¼" seam allowances.

From *each* assorted print, cut:
2 rectangles, 4½" × 8½" (80 total)

From the red print, cut:
5 strips, 9¼" × 42"; crosscut into 20 squares, 9¼" × 9¼". Cut each square into quarters diagonally to make 80 *large* triangles.

10 strips, 2½" × 42"

8 strips, 1½" × 42"

From the white print, cut:
10 strips, 4⅞" × 42"; crosscut into 80 squares, 4⅞" × 4⅞". Cut each square in half diagonally to make 160 *small* triangles.

From the white solid, cut:
17 strips, 3" × 42"

MAKING THE BLOCKS

Sew pieces right sides together. Press all seam allowances as indicated by the arrows.

1. Sew a small white triangle to one short edge of a large red triangle; press. Add a second small white triangle to the remaining edge to make a flying-geese unit; press. The unit should measure 4½" × 8½", including the seam allowances. Repeat to make 80 flying-geese units.

Make 80 units,
4½" × 8½".

2. Sew together a flying-geese unit and a print 4½" × 8½" rectangle to make a quarter-block unit; note that the flying-geese unit should point toward the print rectangle. Press. Repeat to make 80 quarter-blocks.

Make 80 quarter-blocks,
8½" × 8½".

3 Lay out four quarter-blocks in two rows as shown; sew and press. Join the rows to make a block, which should measure 16½" square, including the seam allowances. Repeat to make 20 blocks.

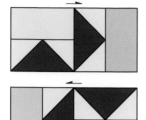

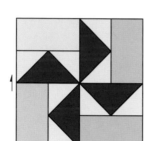

Make 20 blocks,
16½" × 16½".

ASSEMBLING THE QUILT TOP

1 Lay out the blocks in five rows of four blocks per row. Sew the blocks in each row together and press. Join the block rows to complete the quilt-top center, which should measure 64½" × 80½".

2 Sew eight white solid 3"-wide strips together end to end; press the seam allowances open. Measure the length of the quilt top and cut two border strips to this length, which should be 80½". Sew the border strips to the sides of the quilt top. Press.

3 Measure the width of the quilt top, which should be 69½", and cut two border strips to this length. Sew the border strips to the top and bottom edges of the quilt top. Press.

4 To make the middle border, repeat steps 2 and 3 using the red 1½"-wide strips. The side borders should be 85½" and the top and bottom borders should be 71½". Press.

5 To make the outer border, repeat steps 2 and 3 using the remaining white 3"-wide strips. The side borders should be 87½" and the top and bottom borders should be 76½". Press. The quilt top should measure 76½" × 92½".

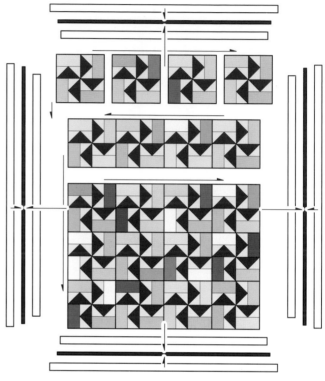

Quilt assembly

FINISHING THE QUILT

For more explanation on any of the finishing steps, go to ShopMartingale.com/HowtoQuilt for free downloadable information.

1 Prepare the quilt backing so it's about 8" larger in both directions than the quilt top.

2 Layer the backing (right side down), batting, and quilt top (right side up). Baste the layers together.

3 Hand or machine quilt; the quilt shown is quilted with an allover orange peel design of interlocking circles.

4 Use the red 2½"-wide strips to make binding and attach it to the quilt.

Designed and pieced by **BONNIE OLAVESON;** machine quilted by **SUSAN HANSEN**

This quilt may look difficult, but it's not! Make the sherbet-colored blocks
in a scrappy array of prints by using 2½" precut strips.

sherbet stars

QUILT SIZE: 84½" × 96½"
BLOCK SIZE: 12" × 12"

MATERIALS

Yardage is based on 42"-wide fabric.

- 6⅓ yards of white print for blocks, setting squares, and borders
- 40 strips, 2½" × 42", of assorted prints for blocks and middle border
- 1½ yards of green print for outer border
- ⅞ yard of aqua print for binding
- 7⅞ yards of fabric for backing
- 93" × 105" piece of batting
- Lightweight template plastic
- Fabric marker

CUTTING

*All measurements include ¼" seam allowances.
Triangle patterns A, B, and C are on page 79. See
"Making and Using Plastic Templates" on page 26
to make plastic templates from the patterns.*

From the white print, cut:

5 strips, 12½" × 42"; crosscut into 15 squares,
   12½" × 12½"

1 strip, 4½" × 42"; crosscut into 4 squares, 4½" × 4½"

21 strips, 2½" × 42"; crosscut into 306 squares,
   2½" × 2½"

8 strips, 4½" × 42"

11 strips, 4½" × 42"; crosscut into 142 A triangles

From *each of 15* assorted print strips, cut:

4 B triangles (60 total)

4 C triangles (60 total)

From *each of 15* assorted print strips, cut:

8 squares, 2½" × 2½" (120 total)

**From the remaining assorted print strips and
scraps, cut:**

15 *pairs* of matching squares, 2½" × 2½" (30 total)

156 squares, 2½" × 2½"

From the green print, cut:

82 B triangles

82 C triangles

From the aqua print, cut:

10 strips, 2½" × 42"

MAKING THE BLOCKS

Sew pieces right sides together. Press all seam
allowances as indicated by the arrows.

1 To make the star-point units, gather B and C
triangles (four each) from one print. Sew a B
triangle and a C triangle to opposite edges of a
white A triangle to make a star-point unit; press.
The unit should measure 4½" square, including
the seam allowances. Make four matching units.
Repeat to make 15 sets of four matching star-
point units.

Make 15 sets of 4 units,
4½" × 4½".

A Trick for Perfect Star Points

The placement of the B and C triangles can be a little tricky. For accurate units, the skinny point of the B and C triangles should extend ½" past the cream triangle. Also, make sure to sew the triangles with the blunt ends at the bottom.

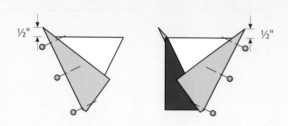

2 To make the corner four-patch units, choose a set of eight matching print 2½" squares. Pair two of the squares with two white 2½" squares. Sew the pieces in two rows as shown; press. Join the rows to make a four-patch unit; press. The unit should measure 4½" square, including the seam allowances. Make four matching four-patch units. Repeat to make 15 sets of four matching corner four-patch units.

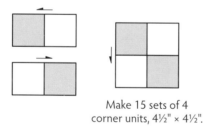

Make 15 sets of 4 corner units, 4½" × 4½".

3 Using two remaining matching print 2½" squares and two white 2½" squares, repeat step 2 to make a four-patch unit. Repeat to make 15 center four-patch units.

Make 15 center units, 4½" × 4½".

4 Lay out four corner units, four star-point units, and one center unit in three rows; make sure the print squares in the four-patch units face the correct direction. Join the pieces in rows; press. Join the rows to complete the block, which should measure 12½" square, including the seam allowances. Repeat to make 15 blocks.

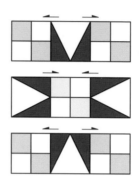

Make 15 blocks, 12½" × 12½".

ASSEMBLING THE QUILT TOP

1 Lay out the blocks and white 12½" setting squares in six rows of five per row, alternating the blocks and setting squares.

2 Sew the pieces in each row together. Press. Join the rows to complete the quilt-top center, which should measure 60½" × 72½".

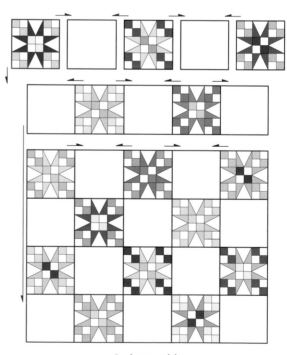

Quilt assembly

Designed and pieced by **BONNIE OLAVESON;** machine quilted by **SUSAN HANSEN**

3 For the inner border, sew the white 4½"-wide strips together end to end; press the seam allowances open. Cut two border strips 60½" long and sew them to the top and bottom edges of the quilt. Press. Cut two border strips 80½" long and sew them to the sides of the quilt. Press.

4 To make the middle border, sew a remaining print 2½" square together with a white 2½" square to make a checkerboard unit; press. Repeat to make 156 checkerboard units.

Make 156 units,
2½" × 4½".

5 Join 34 checkerboard units to make a short middle border, which should measure 4½" × 68½", including the seam allowances. Press. Repeat to make a second short border. Sew the border strips to the top and bottom edges of the quilt top. Press.

6 Join 44 checkerboard units to make a long middle border, which should measure 4½" x 88½", including the seam allowances. Press. Repeat to make a second long border. Sew the border strips to the sides of the quilt top. Press.

Make 2 short borders,
4½" × 68½".

Make 2 long borders,
4½" × 88½".

7 To make the outer border, make a star-point unit using green B and C triangles and a remaining white A triangle. Make 82 star-point units.

Make 82 units,
4½" × 4½".

8 Join 19 star-point units to make a short outer border, which should measure 4½" × 76½", including the seam allowances. Press. Repeat to make a second short border.

Join two white 4½" squares and 22 star-point units to make a long outer border, which should measure 4½" × 96½", including the seam allowances. Press. Repeat to make a second long border.

Make 2 short borders,
4½" × 76½".

Make 2 long borders,
4½" × 96½".

9 Sew the short border strips to the top and bottom edges of the quilt top. Press. Sew the long border strips to the sides of the quilt top. Press.

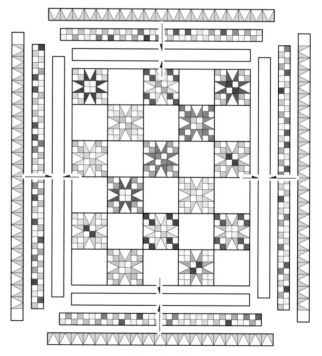

Adding borders